God!

How Could You Let This Happen?

Harvey & Debbie,
Love & Blessings,
Linda Wright

Linda Burge Wright, M.Ed.

…I will never, never fail you nor forsake you.
(Hebrews 13:5 LB)

I cried out. "Chrissy, Chrissy, where are you
baby? Oh God, oh my God, where is she?
You, Father are in control, show them where to
find her!" My cry was soundless, crawling
through my mind. I had already committed
everything to the Lord, I could make no *deals*.

 "Father, every time I open my Bible, it seems
like I read, 'Ask and you shall receive, seek and
you shall find.' I'm asking You to return her
today. If You don't honor your word, I'm not
going to have any faith in You tomorrow."

It wasn't a threat. Just my truth.

Tomorrow dawned without Chris being found.
My first conscious thought was, "This is the day
I have no faith." Yet, even as the thought
flickered across my consciousness, I found
myself looking into a clear manifestation
of the loving Father's presence. No bright lights,
no thunder, not even a praising choir, just such
an awareness of His wonderful Being in that
room. I could neither deny His reality nor His
loving personal care. God would not let me
be lost to Him.

I have included in this book scripture verses mostly quoted and noted from the Living Bible, by Tyndale House Publishers, re-published by Zondervan Publishers. Others are quoted from the Message by Eugene H. Peterson or The Full Life Study Bible, New International Version, Life Publishers International, Zondervan.

Many of the pertinent Scriptures that provide the answers in Chapter 21 are the work and research done by Pastor Tim Isley in preparation for his sermon at Carolina Christian Community Church in Asheboro, North Carolina, April 1, 2012.

Names with *asterisks have been changed.

Much of this work is composed of excerpts taken from *From Chrysalis to Christ,* by Linda Wright

In memory of Christine Marie Wright

7

Want immediate answers? Go to Chapter 21

Publish His glorious acts throughout the earth!
Tell everyone about the amazing things He
does!
For the Lord is great beyond description,
And greatly to be praised!
(Psalms 96:3 LB)

1

And now just as you trusted Christ to save you,
trust him, too, for each day's problems;
live in vital union with him. Let your roots grow
down into him and draw up nourishment
from him. See that you go on growing in the
Lord and become strong and vigorous in
*the truth you were taught. (*Col. 2:6-7 LB)

"I can't believe it, I slept all night!!" None of our four children, ages four to seven had awakened me, even the dog had stayed quiet through the night. It would be a good day!

Squinting at the clock, I saw that it read 5:45. That meant it was really 5:30. Our clocks were set fifteen minutes ahead to allow for all the unexpected last minute calamities that befall small children when they are being hustled off to babysitters and schools on a schedule. This way too, I could cheat just a little, not getting up right on the alarm, but taking a moment to adjust to the claims the day's schedule would be making in the next few hours.

Mentally I checked off a list of things I knew needed to be done. "Were my lessons in order? Did I have any worksheets to run off this morning? No, That was taken care of before I left yesterday." I promised to take Chrissy to see our new house. She had been so disappointed when we couldn't go yesterday and had drawn an array of pictures, her images of what it would be like. Colorful flowers bloomed at each window.

Ever since last Friday when we announced to the children that we had signed papers purchasing a home, Chris had badgered us to take her to see it. With visions of a room all her own, she was in for the disappointing news that she would still be sharing quarters with her younger sister, Theresa.

Theresa was not noted for keeping things in order, and Chrissy, the organizer she was, found it hard to understand why a four year old could not assume the same responsibility for cleanliness as a seven year old. Admittedly, much of the cleanup fell unfairly on the older daughter's shoulders.

Tuesday had been a busy day, and on the way home that afternoon after teaching a group of fourth graders a religious instruction class at St. Mark's Catholic Church, I had decided to let the trip wait until tomorrow.

Yes, Tuesday had been a busy day and today carried with it the prospect of a similar routine.

Theresa's medication for her epilepsy needed to be refilled, and I wondered in fact if her dosage didn't need some adjusting. "Did Kenny have Indian Guides today? No, that would be Thursday. Today is Wednesday…"

Wednesday, February 13, 1974

Whew! Was there no relief? "Maybe I should do like the mother in last night's TV special and run away. "Ha!" I had to chuckle, admittedly, there were times when I wished I could just stop the clock and the clamor, but I loved it here with these four bright lively children and my strong, sensible, gentle, often silly husband. I pulled the covers over my head to grab one last wink before attacking the day and the clink of dishes from the tiny apartment kitchen told me Ken was fixing breakfast. A smile at his thoughtfulness nudged me further awake, and I luxuriated the extra minute his kitchen activities gave me and enjoyed the warmth his love cut through the February chill.

I thought of the changes he had brought to my life.

Thirteen years earlier, I had taken the habit of a Sister in a Dominican convent in Grand Rapids, Michigan. After five years of enjoying the peaceful environment and educational blessings

13

that life provided me, I came to believe that God had another plan for my life.

I was not unhappy, there just seemed to be a need for something more. At twenty-five years of age, I considered my best options for marriage were behind me. I was way too old! So that was not my goal. In fact I didn't really have any goal but God's will for me.

I was a teacher, I had a profession that could support me and was willing to see where God would lead.

I joined my family in California. Eight months later, I met Ken, discovered I wasn't past my prime after all and realized what a catch he was.

We married July 2, 1965. Chrissy was born ten months later. Kenny, David and Theresa followed in quick succession.

Smog was a big problem in California, causing our little ones to rotate bacterial infections with considerable consistency. This issue came to a head one day when I took the children on a ride to the beach in San Clemente hoping for some relief from the constant gray haze.

As we drove down the freeway, we came unexpectedly into a desert/ocean cross-draft of clear air. All five of us simultaneously felt and heard our lungs expand and suck in the fresh air. One year old, David, with a surprised look on his face, exclaimed, "What was THAT?!"

That was the deciding factor for me. I thought, "When my baby gets a breath of fresh air and wants to know what it is, it is time to move out of the smog!

It wasn't difficult to get Ken to agree.

We left California for North Carolina and stayed in a little house on his family's property for six weeks while Ken found a job with Avco Finance Company. They located us in the Charleston South Carolina area.

I was hired to teach reading in the sixth grade elementary school of Summerville, and we enjoyed everything but the humidity there for a year.

2

We need have no fear of someone who loves us perfectly. (I John 4:18 LB)

It's critically important at this juncture to recognize a significant change in my perception and relationship with God during our time in South Carolina.

I had functioned thus far with a somewhat negative awareness of Him as a God Who was keeping score of my faults, and I was committed to doing my best not to offend Him.

Donnie Dunphy, a dear friend I left back in California sent me some literature that changed that mind set completely.

It outlined the scriptural basics that convinced me He was, in fact, a God of Love.

Ephesians 1:11 (Living Bible translation) says. "Because of what Christ has done for us, we have become gifts to God that *He delights in."*

"He delights in me?! Like I do my babies! What a novel concept!"

Further, in the Book of John (John 17:23 LB), Jesus prays for us promising to provide all we need for growth in truth and holiness and closes with the words, "that they (they included me) will know You (the Father) sent me, and that *You love them as much as You love me."*

"He loves me as much as He loves Jesus!" That is a lot to comprehend.

All the *rules* are there to protect and guide me.

He loved me enough to step down from His place in heaven to let me know He loved me, even to die for me.

In the coming year, I would get an inkling of just what, in fact, it cost the Father to allow His Son die for us.

3

...Every moment You know where I am.. You both precede and follow me and place your hand of blessing on my head... I can never be lost to your Spirit!...
(Psalms 139:3 and 7 LB)

Avco offered Ken a different office in Richmond, Virginia in July of 1973. He accepted the offer and we made another move.

We found an apartment in Chester, Virginia, about ten miles south of Richmond.

Ours was a typical apartment floor plan with a small kitchen to the left of the front entryway. Stairs to the right led to two upstairs bedrooms. One faced the front parking lot while the other looked out over a walkway between the rows of apartments. We assigned the front room to the girls and the boys were happy to claim the back. A short hallway and bathroom separated them. The living area included a dining area in one corner and sliding glass panels that opened out on a partially fenced patio. To the left of the living area was a small hallway leading to a closet, bathroom and a large master bedroom.

I was satisfied with this arrangement, especially when it became evident we could hear the children through the heat vents when they were playing in their rooms.

They enjoyed exploring their new digs and were happy to start school in this new community. I was able to land a job with the Chesterfield County School System.

I remember wondering if in making so many moves, there would be anyone to stand by us should anything should happen to us.

I found out.

The hands on the clock were creeping dangerously close to 6:00. Glancing around the room, I groaned at the disarray. An extra week of vacation before Christmas provided by a generous snow fall had given me time to catch up on my housekeeping chores and realize how much I was missing by ignoring our little ones in order to get *everything* done.

I had made a conscious decision to let things be until after they went to bed, then do what I could before I crashed for the night.

It was a mess, but I have been glad I gave them that time. Especially when I read one of the papers Chrissy had written for her teacher about what she did when she got home. "When I get home, mom says, Get out of the house."

OUCH!! I wondered what that teacher must think of me!

I crawled out of the bed, threw the covers over the pillows and headed for the kitchen.

Four year old Theresa was still asleep on the couch next to the sliding glass doors. Due to a need to monitor her nocturnal epileptic seizures, we had relaxed our no kids in our bed policy and had allowed Theresa to crawl in next to me at night. It was important to me to be aware of her seizure activity.

She had recently seemed to be pretty well under control and we had insisted that she not continue this practice. Frequently, she would come downstairs and opt for the next nearest substitute, the couch in the living area.

Lately, we would find the sliding glass doors leading to the back patio cracked open and I would often find Theresa with her diapers pulled down to her knees. I assumed they might have been damp and uncomfortable and credited her with tugging them down herself.

She denied opening the doors we conscientiously locked every night. I thought maybe in her half-asleep state, she might not have remembered.

This morning was no different.

Eggs, toast and juice on the table, Ken had gone upstairs to wake the children and reappeared confronting me in the hallway.

"Where's Chris?"

"I don't know, where's Chris?" I replied with a twinkle. A couple of days earlier, she had come down early to hide from her dad so she could jump out and surprise him. I glanced past Ken to realize that again the patio door was open and a cold draft was wafting across Theresa's little bare bottom. I momentarily forgot Ken's question and moved to close the sliding glass door.

As I reached to pull the curtains out of the way, a kind of electrical force seemed to stop me. A mental camera buzzed in my head and captured the imprint of a fist at the top where someone else's hand had pulled them across the open door!

The instant passed, I lifted the curtains back, slid the door shut and turned to check on how chilled Theresa had become. Surprisingly, I found her warm in spite of the icy weather outside.

Then, realizing that Chrissy had not been where we expected her to be, I returned to the door and slid it wide again. I looked out into the still black morning while the impact of Ken's question crawled cautiously into my awareness.

"Chris?" I spoke into the icy darkness. Had she wandered out?

"Are you sure she's not upstairs?" I asked Ken.

"Are you sure she's not hiding down here somewhere?" he countered.

A slow panic began to close my throat. Could she be sleepwalking? Could she have had an epileptic seizure like Theresa and wandered off in a daze? With those thoughts, I returned to the door again to call.

"Chris?"

We contacted our friends in the apartment behind us and my co-teacher, Sonny, who also lived in our apartment complex with his new wife. He set out immediately to join Ken in a search of the apartment area.

Ken stepped out the door and turned around, "Do you have a blanket or something?"

"There's one on Chrissy's bed."

He returned with her blanket and set out to find his daughter. "It's cold out there." he clipped grimly.

Thinking surely she would be found momentarily, I fed our other three, dressed them for school and the babysitter and prepared a plate for Ken and Chrissy.I braced myself for another mad dash to get to school on time. "Of course, Ken would find her."

Time dragged on, Sonny appeared at the door to tell me he'd met our principal on the street and notified him that I'd be running late. "Was it that late?! She should've been found by now. Where was Ken? Why hadn't he come back with Chris? There must be a reasonable explanation for this. There's got to be a logical explanation for this."

Sonny offered to take the children to their babysitter on his way to school and assured me our classroom was covered and everything would be alright. I bundled up Kenny, David and Theresa and packed them off in Sonny's car; then turned back to an empty apartment.

Light was spreading across the sky promising a clear, but icy cold day.

It was February 13, the day before Valentine's Day.

I picked up my full length wool coat and headed out across the icy patio. I waited for some sense of direction, but none came. I began walking, calling out, I headed through the snow, behind the next row of apartments, across a field.

The sun came up and crystallized the whiteness and beauty around me. "She'll be so cold if she's out here now!"

In the frigid sharpness of the morning, my imagination saw me scooping her up, wrapping her up in my coat with me. By the time I had crossed several fields and was numb with cold, I wanted nothing more than to take that coat off and wrap Chrissy in its warmth.

I returned to the apartment around nine o'clock. The police arrived about the same time. We had agreed to call them by seven if we hadn't found our daughter. They asked me to stay in the apartment, so I would be there if/when she was found.

4

Oh Death where is your victory? Oh Death
where is your sting?
(I Cor. 15:55 LB)

I was alone to review events up to the present.
Ken hadn't found her, Sonny's generous
willingness to help and cover my responsibilities
at school,

Our neighbor's thoughtful pot of steaming hot
coffee,

Seeing Kenny, David and Theresa off with
Sonny,

The brief exchange with the police…

I settled down to wait and pray… or try to pray.
Aware of God's all encompassing knowledge, all
I could say was, "I trust You. I trust You."

I was beyond devastated, aware of how little I
deserved the privilege of raising this beautiful,
gifted little girl, I sat numbly in the corner of our
gold naugahyde couch watching the first hours
of an interminable progression of days and
nights, expecting Chrissy's happy little face to
appear any minute at the patio door. As time
wore

on, my expectant image changed to one of Chrissy being carried up to that door, then back to her walking up on her own.

But, how could she? She wore nothing but her thin little cotton nightie. "Are they giving her a blanket to keep warm?" The ominous *they* crept into my thoughts without my fully realizing its implication. "What could be happening to her?

Was she cold? Oh, God!" The groping gasp was soundless, spoken only in my mind.

I tried not to think about what might really be happening to her. Nobody would hurt such a sweet child…

An electric restlessness seized me. I rose and began pacing desperately back and forth across the room. I leaned my hand against the dining room table and felt an indescribable static pressure against the back of my head and neck, enough that it bowed me forward.

Simultaneously, a ripping sensation tore back and forth inside my abdomen.
The letters R-A-P-E impressed themselves on my mind. I knew this was happening to Chris. Staggered by the impact of it, I sank into the nearest chair and dropped open my Bible. The

words,

"Oh death, where is your victory, oh death, where is your sting?" stood out on the page in red print.

Quickly, I flipped to another page, but everything else was unreadable. Tears blurred my vision and my thinking. I closed my Bible and placed it on the arm of the chair. A gutteral groan silently agonized its way through my being while my insides contorted with the awful realization of what had just happened.

"Nooooo."

That agony convulsed its way through the following weeks of denial and later through its confirmation in reality.

Even with confirmation from scripture, I willed it not to be so, pretend it didn't happen; I continued to watch and wait. Several hours after this incident, I felt like I couldn't breath, yet I could. I knew in my heart she couldn't breathe. It was over...

For Chris...

His loved ones are very precious to Him and He Does not lightly let them die. (Psalms 116:15LB)

5

Dear friends don't be bewildered or surprised
when you go through the fiery trials
*ahead… (*I Peter 4:12 LB)

As the day lengthened and people began
returning home from work, the apartment began
filling up with friends and the police began to
take more seriously the possibility that Chris had
been kidnapped.

Detective Pekancy* and Detective Doe* of the
Chesterfield County Police Department had
been assigned to our case and were introduced.

Detective Pekancy acknowledged the
introduction with a reserved nod and a
calculating expression while Doe, who's tough
exterior belied the tears brimming in the corners
of his eyes when he took my hand and promised
to catch whoever took Chris or die trying.

They began a series of questioning techniques
that was to extend intermittently through many
days and even months ahead. The FBI joined
them, given the possibility this could be related
to Ken's job with a finance company.

"What was she wearing? Are any of her things

missing? How old is she?" In my traumatized state of mind, I could not remember how old my daughter was!

Seven? Eight? I told them eight, but she was seven, looking forward to being eight in May. I got it right the next day.

Numbers mysteriously confounded me. It was years before I could effectively balance my checkbook.

"How long have you been married? Who were your boyfriends before Ken? Could any of them think they might be Chrissy's father??? This last question was treated and repeated in countless ways promising as much discretion as possible if this were the case.

"No, no one else could think they were her father." Given the current freedom of sexual mores, this was hard for them to believe; I'm sure there was hope that there was a more benign reason for her disappearance as well.

Documents of our marriage and Chrissy's birth certificate were produced to their satisfaction.

As the questioning progressed, I began to shiver uncontrollably. Sergeant Walker* from the FBI ended the questions protectively, asserting I'd had enough.

I didn't want to stop. I wanted them to find some direction, some clue, but they closed their notebooks and left me alone.

I resumed my wait huddled again on the couch while hypothetical solutions, anxious speculations, references to other cases with plausible similarities bounced back and forth across the room only half glancing off my conscious thought.

TV crews came in to interview us, and hoping to appeal to the possibility of a sympathetic kidnapper or witness, we grabbed every chance we could get to air our plea for our daughter and get her picture into the news.

At that time, there was no national network to display her image in case she were taken across State lines. Try as we might, the only way would have been to streak naked across some campus with her picture in hand. Or for Ken to suddenly try to go o his professional job with very long hair! That was what national news was picking up on in those days.

Our appeals did not result in any links to Chrissy, but it did reach into the hearts and homes of many Virginians. We received hundreds of letters and gifts.

Within hours, our table was piled two feet deep with food I thought sure would go to waste. As it turned out, it was much needed and appreciated by the many who searched from dawn to dark. Five and a half months after we moved here, this community overwhelmingly answered my question about someone standing by us.

An overflow of food was taken to a nearby community center where a communications depot was set up and the search became more organized and systematic. Helicopters were assigned to criss cross the county.

We gladly gave permission for a thorough search of our apartment, hopeful some clue might be found. It never occurred to us that we could be prime suspects, even when Ken and I were asked to take lie detector tests. It stood to reason that they should consider us, so we were more than willing to do whatever we could to settle their minds about us. Then they could move on to whoever did this. We readily agreed.

6

Truth stands the test of time; lies are soon exposed. (Proverbs 12:19 LB)

Riding down to the police headquarters in Richmond with the FBI's Sergeant Walker*, I found myself in a new casually calculated conversation.

"You say you were born in Grand Rapids and went to East Grand Rapids High School?"

"No, I was born in Detroit, but I did go to East Grand Rapids High School."

"You moved to California a year after you left the convent?"

"No, I moved to California right away after I left the convent."

This went on all the way to our destination; each question including some small piece of misinformation. I recognized his tactics pretty quickly, but was too numbed to point out that I was aware of what he was doing. I just continued to answer and correct, realizing he had really done his homework to be able to recall so many minute details of my life.

In time we arrived at our destination and were ushered into a large utilitarian waiting area with metal chairs lining the walls. A counter partitioned off a few desks and a work area secured on end of the room. A large generic clock hung above the door and the reeking smell of stale cigarette smoke permeated the air.

I was seated and left to wait for what seemed a long time, but that's all I had to do anyway. Wait. Finally I was motioned into an adjacent office inhabited by the officer who was to administer the lie detector test.

This chamber consisted of a couple of small chairs, a large desk, a bookshelf full of various types of legal looking books. On the other end of the room, a large *electric* chair faced away from the desk and toward a wall. The interrogated would have his back to the interrogator. A *mirror* was built into the wall just above eye level. I stared up at it, not really aware, just numb with disbelief that all this was really happening, and was instantly assured that no one was on the other side watching me.

Oh, it was an observation window. Of course, somebody would be watching.

The examiner explained each question that

would be asked and demonstrated how the straps from the chair would be attached to my fingers, arms and chest where they would monitor any flight reactions generated by fear (in this case fear of being caught in a lie). He then left me alone, presumably to mull over the questions and get nervous about the test. I don't know.

About a half hour later, he came back, strapped me into the chair, attached electronic receivers to each of my fingers and proceeded to ask the exact questions he had covered with me earlier.

When it was over, a much more relaxed Sergeant Walker took me to lunch and admitted that he had believed I'd had something to do with Chrissy's disappearance. I wasn't hysterical as he would have expected me to be. We seemed to be too unemotional. I was able to tell him that I was absolutely sure God knew exactly where she was and was with her no matter what.

7
I can do all things through Christ who
*strengthens me. (*Phil. 4:13 LB)

Awareness came flooding in with a start. The
sleeping pill the doctor had given me would
normally have worked its magic, but after three
hours, I was wide awake. Too alert for the
possibility of any further escape from the awful
reality that now broke into my thoughts.

 "Oh,God! Please bring her back! I can't wait
another day!"

The very idea that not knowing could go on for
days, was an unbearable prospect.

A voice spoke in my consciousness, "Can you
wait three days?"

"Oh no…"

"Can you wait a week?"

"No, No…" It was a groan.

"How about three weeks?"

"No! No! No…" My insides convulsed with the
impossible sentence God was presenting.

Too distraught to be impressed with the realization that God had answered me, I doubled over the edge of to bed to restrain the turmoil inside.

But, He didn't say she would be found in three weeks, only could I wait that long. It seemed like forever from the edge of the bed.

I think God was helping me to understand that while I couldn't bear to wait that long, I could do all things through Christ who strengthens me.

As the inner sense of convulsion abated, I rose from Chrissy's bed where I had chosen to rest, and headed down the stairs. Ken came out of the kitchen where he had been having coffee with Lieutenant Welton who had kept watch with him through that night. He met me at the foot of the stairs. His comforting arms held my hopeless question.

"Have they found her yet?"

"No, it's only five o'clock; you haven't slept much, why don't you go back up and see if you can sleep a little more? They won't start searching until it gets light out." I couldn't.

Lieutenant Welton stood up to leave and join his

companion on watch in the dark cold night. He was a tall gentle man of strength and compassion, worthy of his profession and the uniform he wore. He was one of only a few who remained straightforward and undeceitful. Later, one of the few officers we were able to feel we could trust. We were confounded as things progressed, not realizing that lies and distortions of the truth were common tactics used to psych suspects into making misstatements and even cave in and confess.

It never occurred to us that the police, the good guys, would lie. We were so

naïve.

The Lord is close to those whose hearts are breaking; … The good man does not escape all troubles – he has them too, but the Lord helps him in each and every one.
(Psalms 34:18 – 19 LB)

8

*The Lord is watching everywhere and keeps His
eye on both the evil and the good.*
(Proverbs 15:3 LB)

The search got under way with the first glimmer
of light, and today there was no procrastination.
Search parties had been organized and every
available officer was called on duty. People in
the community joined in the two or three hours
before they went to work and returned after their
work day was completed.

Some forfeited their days wages, while other
businesses excused their employees so they
could participate in this desperate search for our
little girl.

We all knew with every hour her chances of
survival in that biting February cold were
dwindling.

The compassion demonstrated by the people of
Chester Virginia and its surrounding community
would renew any man's flagging faith in
mankind. Their dedication, efforts and self
sacrifice spoke volumes about their generosity
and concern. Many teachers in our school
system offered to donate their sick days so I
wouldn't be financially penalized by my

absence. The Chesterfield County School System instead voted to give me whatever days I needed.

Ken's assistant manager covered Ken's duties. The flood of food, gifts, offers to help watch the children were overwhelming. Our babysitter, Marie Graham, in fact, took on the responsibility of caring for Kenny, David and Theresa from dawn til dark, keeping them away from the chaotic maelstrom of activity at our apartment and sparing them the frenetic atmosphere and hysterical speculations of well meaning bystanders.

Marie provided an environment of normalcy and was exactly what they needed.   They weren't exposed to the interrogations, the police, National Guard and search crews trooping through the apartment or the huge blood hound track dog, the futile finger printing procedures followed three days after hundreds of people had moved in and out through the sliding glass doors.

They were shielded from the hostility I encountered when after a couple of days, I took Chrissy's bedclothes to the laundry so I could provide her with a clean bed if she were returned to us. No, I didn't think about washing away clues any more than they thought to look for them until it was too late.

39

Television crews interviewed us in the hope they could reach someone who might know something.

The search covered every square inch of the 446 square miles of Chesterfield County. Years later, the *chuk, chuk, chuk* of a low flying helicopter never failed to revive a flood of icy gut wrenching loss in me.

All I knew, amid this impossible insanity, was that Jesus was a reality, not an abstraction, a living hope, my rock, our Savior… and that He loved my Chrissy even more than I did.

9

Not one sparrow… can fall to the ground without your Father knowing it. And the very hairs of your head are numbered. So don't worry! You are more valuable to Him than many sparrows. (Matt. 10:29-30 LB)

Ken stepped in the door, his face ashen with anxiety and lack of sleep. We both realized how impossible it was becoming for Chrissy to have survived the past three days of cold weather. The current persistent wet sleet spelled sure doom for our daughter. If there were any chance she might have survived this long, exposure to the inclemency of today's weather was a death knell.

He slumped into a chair at the dining table, his hair stiff with ice and muttered, "Linda, get me something to eat. I thought I was going to pass out. If I do, I won't be any good to anybody."

I fixed him a toasted cheese sandwich and took the hair dryer to his crystallized hair, mentally noting how little time had elapsed since his bout with the flu and knowing it would make no difference if I suggested he stay in. I kept my admonition to myself. I couldn't bear for him to give up the search. I didn't even have the presence of mind to offer him a hat. I held him for a moment.

When I released him and stepped back, I found myself looking into two cavernous dark coals of fire. The intensity of the agony in his soul shown through his eyes in an almost supernatural dimension. I have never seen such anguish of spirit, not before and not since.

Ken was a man who had the stamina, patience and persistence to accomplish anything he set his mind to, but his was beyond him. He turned and stepped out the door.

Cold and sleet iced his broken heart to its core. Fear gnawed at his frozen bones. Tears burned, seared his vision as he groped for some sign or evidence of his daughter in the icy wet wilderness. His probing eyes fell upon a little canary huddled in the snow, nearly frozen. He reached down, picked it up and warmed it in his hands while he searched.

"What was that scripture? 'Not one sparrow (what do they cost? two for a penny?) can fall to the ground without your Father knowing it... the very hairs on your head are all numbered. So don't worry! You are much more valuable to Him than many sparrows.'" (Matt. 10:28-31LB)

After a time, the canary revived and Ken

released it back into its natural element. A peace settled on him. He could go home now. Somehow, he knew Chris was ok.
I saw a transformed Ken come through the door. His face gentle, peaceful, almost smiling, he held me close and spoke in my ear, "She's alright, honey. I know she's alright." Then he slept, curled up like a babe with a smile reposing itself in the corners of his mouth.

"He gives sleep to His beloved." (Ps. 127:2LB)

Because of His kindness, you have been saved through trusting Christ. And even trusting is not of yourselves; it too is a gift from God. (Eph.2:8 LB)

10

...I will never, never fail you nor forsake you.
(Hebrews 13:5 LB)

I cried out. "Chrissy, Oh Chrissy, where are you
baby? Oh God, oh my God, where is she?
You, Father are in control, show them where to
find her!"

My cry was soundless, crawling through my own
heart. I had already committed everything to my
Lord, I could make no *deals.*

 "Father, every time I open my Bible, it seems
like I read, 'Ask and you shall receive, seek and
you shall find.' I'm asking You to return her
today. If You don't honor your word, I'm not
going to have any faith in You tomorrow."
That's all. It wasn't a threat. Just a fact.

Tomorrow dawned without Chris being found.
My first conscious thought was, "This is the day
I have no faith." Yet, even as the thought
flickered across my consciousness, I found
myself looking into a clear manifestation
of the loving Father's presence. No bright lights,
no thunder, not even a praising choir, just such
an awareness of His wonderful Being in that
room, I could neither deny His reality nor His
loving personal care. God would not let me

be lost to Him.

My mind drifted back to the night before Chrissy disappeared. I wondered if she had sensed something was going to happen. I couldn't remember any other time she resisted bedtime, but that night I had caught her perched at the top of the stairs reading by the bathroom light. She begged to be allowed to stay up, but I wouldn't give in. A while later, she marched through the front room headed for her dad. I assumed she was planning to get his permission to stay up. I was sharp with her, sending her back upstairs. How I wished I had gone up to love her and tuck her in. My last words to her were so harsh. Tears choked my heart.

...I saw myself so stupid and so ignorant; I must seem like an animal to You, O God. But even so, You love me! You are holding my right hand! You will keep on guiding me all my life with your wisdom and counsel; and afterwards receive me into the glories of heaven! ... my spirits droop, yet God remains! He is the strength of my heart; He is mine forever! (Psalms 73:22-26)

11

Do not smother the Holy Spirit. Do not scoff at those who prophesy, but test everything that is said to be sure it is true, and if it is, then accept it.
(1 Thes.5:19-21 LB)

…Here is the test; no one speaking by the power of the Holy Spirit of God can curse Jesus, and no one can say "Jesus is Lord," and really mean it, unless the Holy Spirit is helping him.
*(*1Cor. 12:3 LB)

Dearly beloved friends, don't always believe everything you hear just because someone says it is a message from God: test it first to see if it really is. For there are many false teachers around, and the way to find out if their message is from the Holy Spirit is to ask: Does it really agree that Jesus Christ, God's Son, actually became man with a human body? If so, then the message is from God. If not, the message is not from God but from one who is against Christ…
(I John *4:2-3* LB)

Thanks to the prayer group I had been involved with in South Carolina, I was well grounded in the Word when different psychics, seers and spirituals offered their skills or called. Ken and I both took these scriptures seriously and screened carefully those we were willing to listen to. Our primary question was "Who is Lord?" It was amazing how many callers fumbled that question.

One, however, came back with a resounding, "Jesus is Lord. Jesus is the Son of God who died for us to save us from our sins!"

No hesitation there. We asked her to share her message.

"I saw Chrissy in a room with Jesus. She was kneeling in front of Him and He was holding a cup over her head. She's safe with Jesus."

Ken's hope was that she was physically safe, but my heart was assured that she was with the Lord. Why the cup? What did that mean? I had found that God often confirmed His word of prophecy in His Word (the Bible).

I opened Chrissy's little Bible right to Isaiah 51:17-23. She had underlined it.

You have drunk to the dregs the cup of terror and squeezed out the last drop... but listen now to this, afflicted ones - full of troubles and in a stupor (but not from being drunk) - this is what the Lord says, the Lord your God who cares for

His people: See I take from your hands the terrible cup; you shall drink no more from my fury; it is gone at last. But I will put that terrible cup into the hands of those who tormented you and trampled your souls to the dust and walked upon your backs. (Isaiah 51:17-23 LB)

What an odd scripture for a seven year old to underline. What did it mean?

Col. 1:24 (LB) says, *But part of my work is to suffer for you; and I am glad for I am helping to finish up the remainder of Christ's suffering for His body, the church.*

I don't think that means Christ's suffering was incomplete, but that somehow, our sufferings are joined to His and given value, purpose. I heard in these messages a promise of God's hand on the one who had taken her.

As our case dragged on and remained unsolved. I was freed of any need to seek revenge in the months and years to come.

12

Puny man! Frail as breath! Don't ever put your trust in him! (Isaiah 2:22 LB)

This time a call came from one claiming a different kind of power. "You wancher liddle girl? Well I got her… we're wachin yer house so don't try anything. I'll call back at two o'clock." a disconnect buzz.

Chris had been gone two weeks, now, and Ken and I had just been discussing the fact that it might be months or never before we would know what had happened to her. Both of our jobs had been covered and our salaries continued. It seemed responsible to go back to work. It also seemed like giving up.

It was about 9:30 in the morning. The call blasted our world wide open carving out our desperate hope that someone was really going to return Chris to us! The air was charged with fear, anxiety, hope, vulnerability and an almost carnival like atmosphere.

A knock on the door. Ken opened it a crack and furtively passed a note, "Go away, we're being watched!" Some sympathetic neighbor had no idea why we were acting in such a bizarre manner. It was ludicrous really, since if we were

49

being watched, it would've been obvious someone had come to the door. But we were more than distraught and not thinking particularly straight. Ken paced, then went up to the landing of our stairs and proceeded topound a hole through the wall to the apartment next to us, scaring our neighbors half to death.

They called the police, and soon the parking lot was swarming with black and white vehicles. Officers went into the adjacent apartment, where Ken explained to them through the wall what was going on. We were sure, *being watched*, our hopes would be doomed if the police came into our own apartment. Two o'clock came and went, four o'clock. At five o'clock, Ken grabbed up a handful of pickup sticks and dropped them on the table. Anything to occupy our minds. We began the most desperate game we'd ever played in our lives just as the police decided to barge in on us.

That's how they found us. It's no wonder they were so suspicious of us. We were never hysterical, distraught or vengeful, we didn't fit the pattern (whose pattern?), and now this!

But the phone rang again with orders for Ken to be at Peeble's Drug Store* on the corner of Idlewild * and Baker* at six o'clock. Ken was to wait at a phone booth.

"Come alone!"

The atmosphere recharged with the possibility that we just might have our daughter back after all. Ken left in our eight year old Pontiac, not knowing how we might handle a ransom with no money. He waited there with several plainclothes officers on the sidelines until ten PM. By then, the police had been able to trace the call to a local teenager who had nothing better to do than to perpetrate his little joke on us.

When our door opened, I expected to see Chrissy wrapped in her dad's arms. Instead, after twelve hours of frenzied, intense waiting, Ken came in, empty handed, worse, empty hearted. His expression told the whole story before he even uttered a word. Our hopes were obliterated.

We took a few more days to heal, then returned to our jobs on a Monday, almost three weeks after Chrissy disappeared. Our phone was connected to our neighbor's phone in case there might be an important call. The wire taps remained connected and we began our pitiful attempt to take up life where it had left off.

I felt like I was giving up all hope just by the

51

simple act of walking through my classroom door, but reason won out that this was the most responsible action to take. Deep down, I knew Chrissy's fate from that first day.

Kenny, David and Theresa had barely existed in my awareness. I had been so consumed by the turmoil around us. I knew they had been in good hands with Marie Graham. She had guarded and cared for them faithfully the past three weeks along with her own children. No small task! It was time now to start looking out for them myself and their feelings. How was I going to cope with their feelings too, much less this classroom full of children!?

I had left eons ago in another time, another world, another dimension. Twenty eight little third graders came in. Anxious little voices questioned, "Have they found your little girl?" And in a unison of sympathy and heartfelt concern, they took their places and tried to be so….. quiet and so…. Good… for a couple of hours. Then they returned to being normal little eight year olds. It delights me today to remember their efforts; they were so sweet.

Watching them at work, at play, I was overcome again and again with that desolate anguish; my spirit cried out, she should be in her own classroom like all these other normal healthy children, happy little girls, skipping rope, chanting rhymes, skipping around outdoors, untouched, unaffected by my reality. "Where is she? " I agonized silently.

Kenny returned from his first grade class that first day back, his voice quivering as he expressed the difficulty he'd had answering questions about his sister. He didn't want to talk about it. She'd been his closest companion, playmate and confidant.

David and Theresa were not yet enrolled in school, so they'd had a relatively ordinary experience. We were back to normal. At least we were going through the motions of normal.

13

I am sending you out as sheep among wolves.
(Matthew 10:16 LB)

"I can't stand all their joy!" I cried to my friend. I had escaped to the top of the staircase during our weekly prayer meeting. A chorus of praise and joy was being sung and the members of the prayer group were lost in the delight of prayer. My terrible helplessness estranged me from their song, but I didn't want to leave either.

A call for prayer requests brought me back down the steps in a hurry. "I am so bitter!" I choked out. Their prayer removed the lump that had invaded my throat, it seemed like forever. An ensuing prophetic message assured us that Chrissy would be found and returned to us. The prayer group applauded, sure that she would be alive. But for me, while the message rang true with regard to her being found, her well being translated into being home with our heavenly Father.

This particular evening, a visiting minister from Newport News had joined us to speak and share his witness. One of his stories involved a little girl belonging to a missionary couple.

She had demonstrated immense potential for

sharing God's Word and a great personal love for her Savior when she was struck down by an illness and died. No one could quite come to terms with their feelings and God's apparent will to take her.

They were given a vision. The child appeared deep down in a well or a pit, ringed around with ravenous hungry wolves. The hand of God reached down into the pit, picked up the little girl and lifted her up past the ring of wolves and took her to heaven.

He shared another personal experience when he had been deeply in prayer for a beloved Christian sister who was suffering untold agony and torment from an asthma attack that had her at the point of death. All his prayers, belief in God's healing power and claims on God's promises were not producing the miracle of healing he was expecting. Finally, unable to comprehend a loving God who would allow one of His children to suffer so much agony, he was compelled by honesty to speak his truth to God.

"If You're that kind of God, " he prayed, "then I don't want to be your friend." At that, God took him in spirit from his stool in the kitchen, to the doorway of her room. There, he saw her lying on the bed surrounded by flames furling out all around her. Jesus was standing on the other side of the bed, reaching through the flames, holding her hand.

He looked up at our minister and said, "Tom, I love her more than you do." Tom found himself back on his stool in the kitchen, rebuked in love, still not understanding, but unable to deny God's love.

The woman was, in fact, healed thereafter and spent several more years in missionary service.

14

*Most important of all, continue to show deep
love for each other, for love makes
up for many of your faults.* (I Peter 4:8 LB)

Ken and I found ourselves snapping at each
other sarcastically and stopped cold. We sat
down to discuss this new negative behavior,
admitting we were both hurt and taking it out on
each other. This attitude had never been our
norm so easily recognizable.

 Statistics say ninety five percent of marriages
are in trouble after the loss of a child and eighty
percent are ultimately destroyed. I can see why.

We made a mutual commitment to treat each
other with respect, and while we   were
sometimes almost artificially polite to one
another, the effort behind it was genuine and
effective, and I believe it cemented us together
even more than we had been before.

 A day later, our dear friend and mentor, Laura
Sloan, came in and warned us that marriages
were fragile at a time like this and we ought to
get counseling!

We didn't need to do that on behalf of our
marriage but, the pastor of Chester

Baptist Church, William Russ, was our daily mainstay, counselor, intercessor with the police and constant friend.

I cannot imagine how we would have managed without his support, friendship and advice. The assistant principal at the school where I taught, Sheila Leckie, likewise came in and kept our household in order.

When things were at their worst, she took phone calls, kept records of who called or brought gifts and even helped write the thank you s I was too mentally traumatized to concentrate on. Both probably did more than I know. I just know I was incapable of doing much of anything. I tried to pray, I could barely read little patches of scripture, mostly, I just watched the door.

The time approached when our escrow was to close on our house. How could we leave if Chris might somehow find her way back? My best friend lived in the apartment in back of us. Chrissy would know to go there if she couldn't find us. With that consolation we decided to make our move and on a rainy April first, we packed up our children and things and settled into a sturdy little brick home surrounded by apple, plum, cherry, and pear trees, three kinds of nut trees, bushes and even grape vines.

Now, twenty miles from the apartment, nestled in a quiet neighborhood, we began to realize what an upheaval or lives had been in. Visitors had been a daily expectation in Chester. Here it was just us. We began to relearn how to relate to each other again, to become a family… without Chris.

Still, we waited, wondered each day if our world would explode again with the revelation of our daughter's whereabouts.

15

If you delight in me, I'll give you your heart's desires. Ps. 37:4
Ask for anything *using Jesus name… John 15: 7 &16*

I knelt down, laid my Bible on our ornate Chinese altar table situated in front of the picture window in our living room. With one hand on God's Word, I confronted God with the endless progression of days waiting for any information about our child. I spoke, "Father, You have claimed me as Your daughter. You have promised me my heart's desires if I delight in You. (Ps.37:4) You've said ask for anything using Jesus' name (John 15: 7 & 16). You know that I have truly delighted in You. Now, I am standing on your word and your promises, not on any merit of my own. It's You who said these things. Father, it's my heart's desire to have my daughter back. If she's dead in a ditch, I know beyond a shadow of a doubt, that You can raise her back to life. I want her alive, I want her well, I want her with no emotional scars, and I want her now!"

My heart lay naked on that altar next to His Word as I challenged God to keep His word.

His voice came to me. "But you want my will don't you?"

"Yes, but I want my little girl."

"But you want my will don't you?"

"Yes, but I want my little girl."

"But you want my will don't you?"

I put my head down and sobbed, "Yes, but I want my little girl…"

The following day, April 21, 1974, three hunters were drawn by curiosity to a spot some hundred or so yards downstream from their lookout on a bridge where they could see an odd configuration on the surface of the water. They actually climbed out on a log no more than six inches in diameter before they realized it was Chrissy's hair swirling on the surface. She was submerged, lodged under a nearby log.

Headlight beams flashed across our walls as the tires of a heavy police vehicle crunched into our graveled driveway. It was eleven PM, too late for a friendly visit. I knew instinctively this was *it*. They had found her. I hurried down the hall to slip out of my nightgown into my clothes. Ken came in with a deadly serious look on his face. "Hurry, Hon," he mouthed. I couldn't. After waiting all this time, I didn't want to face the news I already knew. I had so dreaded going on forever not knowing; knowing the truth would be a relief but not a sweet one. I went down the hall and knelt on the floor next to Ken's chair.

Our two primary detectives remained silent, a fixed somber expression on their faces. They shook their heads as we looked to them for the news they had brought.

"They think they have found her. We can't be sure until they do dental exrays tomorrow."

"How sure are they?" ken's voice trembled with his effort to remain calm."About 99%" The decided statement made it quite clear there wasn't any doubt.

"Did you see her nightgown? Did it match the material I gave you in February?" They nodded and went on to explain she was badly decomposed, had lain in the creek probably from the first day; she had most likely been raped, but that would be determined the following day with an autopsy. We immediately wanted to go see her, but they discouraged us; it would be too traumatic. Ken deferred, not wanting me to be subject to that kind ofmemory. I deferred, not wanting to put him through that experience. Later, we discussed the reality that we had both really wanted to go, but considered each other. God did spare us at least one sad memory there.

I was numb, literally and figuratively. Later, when I was alone, as the realization of what Chrissy had suffered sank in. A desolate, heart wrenching grief overcame me, and I convulsed in sobs until I ran out of tears. Then, it turned inward.

The rest of the world went on about their business oblivious of the silent agony devouring me.

God did not leave me believing that Chrissy suffered and died alone. At a time when I was thinking with mental images of Christ's suffering, I wondered if I would be willing to lie down on the cross and allow myself to be nailed to it like He did. I quailed at the idea, then consoled myself by thinking even Jesus asked the Father to let that cup of suffering to pass from him. I was still imagining the cross lying before me and thought, but I'd do it for Chrissy if I could! I moved toward the cross. Suddenly, Christ came between me and the cross. He seemed to say, "I already did that." He stood aside, arms and head down and I received, "It's already been done."

HE took Chrissy's pain on the cross…

16
Because He lives, I can face tomorrow…
(Gaither Music)

Early morning light filtered through the blinds
and with it dawned the realization that our long
wait was over. Nine and a half weeks of
suspense. She was really dead… raped…
drowned… How could anyone do that to any
seven year old child? much less, one as sweet
as Chrissy? What kind of sickness, social
injustice could bring a man down to that level?
Another silent convulsive groan agonized itself
through my being.

Ken was awake, silent, his face a grim mask.
There was nothing to say. I reached over, laid
my hand against his arm for a moment, then
rose. It was not even six AM, but there would
be no more sleep. After warming Ken's coffee, I
just stood speechless, empty, aimlessly groping
through the motions of fixing breakfast.

Kenny's footsteps sounded in the hall. I heard
them slow down as he approached his dad.
"What's wrong, Dad?"

"Chrissy's dead."

Kenny came in, buried his head in my lap and
cried, partly from fear, partly from the loss of his

best friend and playmate, partly from the sadness around him. He later admitted his dad's grief struck him the hardest. His understanding of the circumstances of his sister's death was limited. Someone stole her and threw her in a creek where she drowned. She was with Jesus, so it was okay. He was secure in our faith. David and Theresa, likewise followed suit with a simple direct faith and some fascination with the flurry of activity that followed.

By seven o'clock, our Preacher Russ had already driven the twenty miles to be with us and to offer us whatever services he could. He knew and understood the details and arrangements that needed to be made, while we not only were clueless about any kind of planning, but pretty much incapable. He walked us through each step, even offering out of consideration for my Catholic background to have Mass offered at his church.

Sheila Leckie again took up her post as our hostess, telephone operator and all around coordinator, holding our household together.

I went and hid in Theresa's bedroom to sew pitifully on a favorite but too small dress that Chrissy loved and would be buried in. After awhile, I went out to the backyard and hid against the warm brick of our house.

I couldn't bear to hear one more person say, "It's alright, she's with the Lord." Or It's good you have other children."

There was nothing alright about the way she died, and a hundred other children could not take Chrissy's place in my heart.

Pastor Lindquist, a friend of ours stated, "No one else can take your place in Jesus' heart," That resonates so well with how I felt about my daughter… how I feel about each of my children.

I cried out silently, "I'm so sorry! I'm so sorry! Oh, Chrissy!" for the horrifying desecration she endured, for times I had been ridiculously rigid with her. I ached to hold her after her first trip to the dentist had proven painful and I just suggested that she should now brush her teeth more regularly. What would it have hurt to have comforted her? "I'm so sorry, I'm so sorry, Baby!"

Her spirit came to me and rested on my shoulder. It wrapped itself around my face and forgave me everything, loved me.

Now, I could face the events to come, the

agonizing sense of loss coupled with the sure knowledge that *she*, in fact, still lived. She *was* alright.

Late that afternoon, the priest of our parish came by and a decision was made to have an evening Mass said in lieu of a visitation and a formal funeral at Preacher Russ's Baptist Church the following day. Then, Chrissy's body would be sent to *Asheboro*, North Carolina to be buried near Ken's family. We didn't know if we would be staying in Virginia and didn't want to bury her there given the possibility there might one day be no family near her grave. At best, we would be visiting North Carolina on occasion.

We had no concept of the costs of funerals, shipping across State lines, and a third graveside service in Asheboro. We would have been paying for this for a long time had we been charged for these things, but Alvin Small's Funeral Home in Hopewell charged us nothing for all they provided, nor did Ridge Funeral Home in Asheboro. In fact the Chester Florist didn't even charge us for Chrissy's beautiful casket bouquet of roses. To top it off, people in the community donated money for a memorial so we were able to install a suitable grave marker and provide music for the Baptist choir who performed a memorial service of Gaither's

Alleluia Music, every bit as beautiful as the original music sung by their own choirs.

It was during one of the funeral services as I stood about three feet away from our daughter's casket, when I became aware of Chrissy's spirit skipping happily into Jesus arms. I could not tell you any detail about what they were wearing or how Jesus looked, but I was clearly aware of Chrissy with her arms outstretched toward Jesus and He with His arms open to welcome her. The Father's voice spoke again in my mind, "Alright, now ask."

A memory of God's hands holding my face a year earlier as I prayed at my desk in my South Carolina classroom, flooded my senses with the profound joy of belonging to Him.

My request at the altar table came back as well, but seeing Chrissy in Jesus arms, I knew I would never want to take that joy and comfort away from her. I whispered, "No! No! No!"

Blessed assurance! After the service, I remember someone telling me they didn't know how I was able to stand it. I wasn't able to express what I had just seen, but I thought, "If you had only seen what I did, you would understand."

Someday I will be able to hold her again.
It was close to six years before I ever shared
this experience with anyone but Ken, only to be
told perhaps I was so traumatized as to be
delusional. I cried the rest of the day, having
opened up about something so sacred and
priceless to me, but it affirmed its truth to me,
and I have become secure about sharing it with
others.

It has amazed me, once I have shared some of
these spiritual blessings, how many people have
had similar experiences, especially parents who
have lost one of their children.

I even ran it by a psychiatrist, not because I
doubted it, but I wanted to know how a
professional perceived this kind of thing. He
was very clear that such spiritual manifestations
are within the norm of human experience and do
not fall into the category of delusion.

17
Restore to me again the joy of Your salvation…
Then I will teach your ways…
(Psalms 51:12-13 LB)

I returned to the classroom the Monday after the funeral and struggled through May and the first week in June in a blur of unreality. One afternoon, I pulled up to an intersection, stopped at the stop sign, then pulled out right in front of an oncoming car unaware of its presence, just going through the motions.

Another time, I found myself several miles down a road with no memory of driving it. I appealed to some friends to let me car pool for awhile.

My third graders left me little time to dwell on what had happened, but before they arrived and after they left, the heaviness of loss was almost unbearable. At one time, I was listening to a Christian tape encouraging joy. I said, "Father, how can I do that when my heart is so heavy?"

I felt His hand reach inside my chest and squeeze my heart with the message, "I don't want your heart heavy." But it was.

Mid June brought with it the leisure to grieve. I chose to allow myself to wade through it, held Chrissy's memorabilia, imagined her terrified inability to understand what was happening to her in her last moments, the expression on her face, the sound of her cry… the loss of the awesomely beautiful little human being she was.

One day, I was standing outside under our cherry tree, the weather was mild, a soft breeze was blowing, leaves allowed flickers of sunlight to filter through into my line of vision. I thought, "If I hadn't left the convent, I would never hurt this bad." Immediately, It was clear. I wouldn't trade the wonder and joy of having my little Chris for anything in the world! I would accept any amount of grief or pain for the privilege of having known her. No, I had no regrets about that decision in my life.

An anonymous poem read at her funeral speaks to the gift of this child.

"I'll lend you for a little time, a child of mine," He said,
For you to love the while she lives and mourn for when she is dead.
She may be six or seven years or twenty two or three,
But will you til I call her back, take care of her for Me?

I've looked the wide world over in my search for teachers true,
And from the throngs that crowd life's lanes, I have selected you.
Now, will you give her all your love, nor think the labor vain,
Nor hate Me when I come to call to take her back again?"
I fancied that I heard them say, "Dear Lord, Thy will be done.
For all the joy Thy child shall bring, the risk of grief we'll run.
We'll shelter her with tenderness, we'll love her while we may
And for the happiness we've known, forever grateful stay.
But should the angels call for her much sooner than we planned,
We'll bear the bitter grief that comes, and try to understand."

18
Lord, I am overflowing with Your blessings...
(Psalms 119:31 LB)

I looked down at my firstborn, Mother's Day,
1966. Her black hair stuck out in every
direction. Her misshapen head and face, her
beet red complexion gave her wrinkled little face
very little hope of a future favorable
countenance. But I didn't care if she was the
ugliest baby I'd ever seen, I was so in awe of
this miracle of life. I loved her so much!
"Please, God, give her a good personality!"

How could I have known that the lopsided jaw
line, mushed up little head and even the sticking
up black hair would turn into a golden haired,
hazel eyed beauty with the sweet personality I
had prayed for and a compassion, generosity
and sensitivity far beyond her years.

As I dragged through a second, third and fourth
pregnancy, there was Chrissy, patting away my
headache, asking, "Can I get you anything,
Mommy?"

How many times did those chubby little toddler
legs go running up and down the hall
to fetch diapers, pacifiers, Vaseline, baby
powder or any other thing I might have been in

need of? I'd wrap my arms around her and say, "I don't know what I'd ever do without you. I just couldn't live without you!"

I was aware of Chrissy's spirit, throughout that year, as it frequently manifested itself to me. It wasn't something I could make happen; it just happened. How? I don't know. I just know she came to love and comfort me.

A friend had suggested that I needed to let her go. I needed to let her know that after all, I could live without her, and there were better things in store for her. When her spirit settled on the floor facing me, I explored that possibility with her and told her I would be okay.

She stayed awhile longer loving me, then, faded away.

Before Ken, before Chrissy, I never knew such love existed.

19

And we know that all that happens to us is
working for our good if we love God
and are fitting into His plans. (Romans 8:28 LB)

Life in my family was an exercise in survival.
My dad was an exceptionally intelligent and
successful businessman. He was a man of
integrity, honesty and hard work, as well as a
crack shot hunter. He always managed to catch
fish a hair smaller than the ones my mother
caught, but he was the one who taught us
how to clean and prepare fish and game, bait a
hook and, best of all, fly the highest homemade
kite! But his job took him out of town a lot so he
was not aware of the dynamic that existed in his
absence.

My mother believed good discipline consisted of
rejection, shame and physical punishment. At
one time she commented that she used
switches or a belt because they would not break
our bones if she lost her temper. And she did
 lose her temper. If she decided we were lying,
black and white proof could not change her
mind. If I had the wrong look on my face she
might create a reason for it in her mind and
accuse me of something I never thought of.
One incident, especially, took years for me to
come to terms with. I had gone for a
walk in the woods behind our cottage at the lake

with a (boy) friend. We were both totally naïve, eleven or twelve years old. (Yes, Back in the early fifties, it was still possible to be naïve at that age.) We were sweet on each other, but not even at a holding hands stage. We just enjoyed the mysteries of the woods, and had built a little twig house under a tree. When we returned, my mother went into a total rage, taking a belt to me, backing me up against a woodpile, lashing at me until I thought I was separating from my body. When she had no more strength, she stopped and scolded me not to go around showing people my bruises so they would feel sorry for me.

Years later, I came to realize that there was a reason my great grandmother had stood guard by her bedroom door when she was a child and her parents were lost in their alchoholic world. And there was a reason for her need to find a focus for the indwelling rage and bitterness that threatened to consume her.

My five years in the convent, away from that punitive dynamic and subject to a positive one was beyond price when it came to establishing a loving environment for our children, not to mention the insight it gave me as a teacher when troubled children were assigned to my classroom. I'm so grateful for the countless ways God has blessed me in these experiences.

When we made our funeral arrangements for Chrissy, my mother, in her inability to face it, decided that I contrived to keep information about the arrangements from her because I didn't want her to come. I had waited until they were complete before I called her, but she decided we didn't want her to know what they were and informed my sister and my two brothers that I did not want them around.

She called me at two o'clock in the morning, the day of the funeral accusing me of manipulating to keep them all away.

When I hung up the phone, I could only wonder how a mother could do that to a daughter; but I was already so heartbroken over our baby, I was impervious to any more hurt. Her refusal to come was a blessing. I was too numb, too overwhelmed with current reality too concerned about Kenny, David and Theresa to focus on her non-presence, much less take the cautions that would've been necessary given her sensitivities and bitterness.

20

I am the true Vine and my Father is the Gardener. He lops off every branch that doesn't produce. And He prunes those branches that bear fruit for even larger crops. He has already tended you by pruning you back for greater strength and usefulness by means of the commands I gave you. Take care to live in Me and let me live in you. For a branch can't produce fruit when severed from the vine. Nor can you be fruitful apart from Me. (John 15:1-5 LB)

"You've pruned me back too far!" I cried. Life felt like it was over for me. I visualized a large cut down so all that was left was a stump. That's how I felt, like a stump. There was nothing left, no joy, no witness; my world had collapsed into inconsolable grief. I felt like I had been killed right along with my child.

Two friends appeared at the door. One, Mary*, had recently lost her little two year old when her husband's gun went off while he was cleaning it. The other was Betty, our Preacher Russ's wife, a jovial, loving, supportive friend. As we sat together, our conversation turned to our commonality of Faith. My Catholicism, while liturgical, hierarchical and highly doctrinal still adhered to faith in a Triune God (Father, Son and Holy Spirit), faith that Jesus was sent to us by the Father to die for our sins and redeem us back into a loving relationship with the Father.

I was able to share my experience in the charismatic movement in a way that enlightened them about some of the gifts of the Spirit that are promoted by the Spirit-filled movement, sometimes in a radical, pushy, divisive manner.

Betty, our Preacher's wife had been injured by some of the problems caused in their church by overly zealous charismatics. Bottom line, the Holy Spirit's work in our lives is to bring us to Jesus.

For an enlightening instant, I glimpsed the image of a barren stump sprouting a single healthy happy leaf... promise of growth to come.

21

...For God is greater than man. Why should you fight against Him just because He does not give account to you of what He does? (Job 33:12-13 LB)

Because of His kindness, you have been saved through trusting Christ. And even trusting is not of yourselves; it too is a gift from God. (Eph. 2:8 LB)

Truth be known, in spite of all the ways God had assured me of His presence, love and action in our lives, I still cried out, "Why didn't You prevent this! How Could You Let This Happen!

Why didn't You send your angels to protect her!" My "Why? Why? Why? was tinged with a sense of betrayal. "I trusted You. How could You let this happen?"

Ken and I slept in fear, with bells strewn across the hall so no one could sneak into our children's bedrooms. A bow and arrow lay by Ken's side of the bed and a toy gun next to me. We fenced in the area under our bedroom windows and put a beautiful white American Eskimo dog in that space to guard it.

As I became acquainted with the book of Job, it became clear that God was God and ultimately didn't have to answer to me. With this understanding, I was given such a sense of His love, that instead of feeling rebuked, I was open to accept His truth. My job was to continue to trust Him.

Let me be clear, I fully believe God is not offended by any honest prayer, including the asking of why. He tells us to pray about everything. It is just possible I was somewhat demanding… Ahem.

Solomon, in all his wisdom grappled with the same kinds of questions, along with Job and King David.

Job said, "I am innocent, but I don't know what to think… God destroys the innocent as well as the guilty… Is it God who keeps the leaders from seeing when an evil person takes control? If it is not God, who is it?" (Job 9:21 – 24)

Uh, might it be Satan?? (me)

Solomon said, "I looked long and hard at what goes on around here, and let me tell you, things are bad…" (Eccl. 6:1)

David said, "Look at these wicked people – enjoying a life of ease while their riches multiply. Did I keep my heart pure for nothing? Did I

keep myself innocent for no reason? I get
nothing but trouble all day long… "
(Ps.73: 12 – 13)
"I almost slipped and lost my balance, I almost
fell into sin. I saw that wicked people were
successful and I became jealous…"
(Ps. 73:2 – 3)
"I wanted to tell others these things, but that
would have made me a traitor to Your people. I
tried hard to understand all this, but it was too
hard for me. But then, God, I went to Your
temple, and I understood what will happen to
the wicked. I was so stupid… God, I was upset
and angry with You! … You hold my hand.
You lead me and give me good advice, and
Later You will lead me to glory. God, I have only
You. And if I am with You, what on earth could I
want? God, people who leave You will be lost…
all I need is to be close to God."
(Ps. 73: 15 – 28)

Solomon, after trying out experiments with work,
pleasure, wealth and possessions concluded, "It
is all meaningless." (Eccl. 2) …the end of the
matter is: Fear God (revere and worship Him,
knowing that He is.) and keep His
commandments, for this is the whole of man
(the full, original purpose of His creation,
 the object of God's providence,
the root of character,
the foundation of all happiness,

the adjustment to all inharmonious circumstances and conditions under the sun) and the whole (duty) for every man." (Eccl. 12:13)
"God has planted eternity in men's hearts and minds... (Eccl 3:11)

Later, the apostle Paul writes, "For ever since the world was created, people have seen the earth and sky. Through everything God made, they can clearly see His invisible qualities – His eternal power and dIvine nature. So they have no excuse for not knowing God. Yes, they knew God, but they wouldn't worship Him as God or even give Him thanks... they began to think up foolish ideas of what God was like, as a result, their minds became dark and confused..." (Romans 1:20 – 22)

I'm not so sure I wasn't teetering on the brink of just such a mistake, believing that because I had given over my trust to God, He would not allow anything bad to befall us. I had established my own set of expectations. God did not come down and squeeze Himself into my standard. Hmm. But He clearly continued to love and save me.

The apostle Peter writes, "Don't be bewildered or surprised when you go through the fiery trials ahead, for this is no strange unusual thing that

is going to happen to you." (I Peter 4:12)
"…let Him have all your worries and cares, for
He is always thinking about you and watching
everything that concerns you. Be careful –
watch out for attacks from Satan, your great
enemy. He prowls around like a hungry roaring
lion, looking for some victim to tear apart. Stand
firm when he attacks. Trust the Lord; and
remember that other Christians around the
world are going through these sufferings too.
(I Peter 5:7 – 9)

Ultimately, God did not spare His Son the
desecration and humiliation of the cross, why,
then should I be exempt from the effects of
fallen man? Hmm.

"…Now, teach me good judgment as well as
knowledge…

You are good and do only good."
(Psalms 119:65 LB)

22

(Titus 3:1&2 LB) *Remind your people to obey the government and its officials and always be obedient and ready for any honest work.*

Then, (Romans 13:1-3 LB) *Obey the government for God is the one who put it there. There is no government anywhere that God has not placed in power. So those who refuse to obey the laws of the land are refusing to obey God, and punishment will follow. For the policeman does not frighten people who are doing right, but those doing evil will always fear him.*

Ken agreed to a third polygraph, though he had clearly passed the first two. Two detectives picked him up at his office the following Thursday and drove him to Newport News some sixty miles away. Authorities there had acquired a reputation for breaking suspects down and getting them to sign confessions after some degree of bullying. At the time we knew nothing of it.

In Newport News, one officer played the role of the good guy, "We'll help you, we'll get you the help you need." The other affirmed that he knew Ken was guilty, that he'd failed the lie detector test miserably and he'd better confess.

They implied to him that I had been having affairs behind his back. They took turns trying to break him throughout the afternoon and on into the night. Ken finally told them to either arrest him or take him home.

Legal statutes there maintain that a suspect cannot be held more than twelve hours. Ken was returned home after 2 AM. He walked in, put his head on my shoulder and told me, "A lesser man would have confessed." He was heartbroken. He didn't know that I had been called down to headquarters in Chesterfield while he'd been gone.

Rise up, O Lord my God; vindicate me. Declare me "not guilty," for You are just.
(Psalms 35:23 LB)

I walked into a room full of officers openly packing their guns and a comment timed to my entry, "Well if that's true, then *she's* an accessory. Uh Oh." like he was surprised I had walked in. They escorted me down a hall to a room where I was read my rights and offered a lawyer, which I did not feel I needed. I still believed in the *good guys.* I was told that they were absolutely sure that Ken had killed our daughter, that he was a psychotic, that he had caused the needle of the lie detector test to scatter all over the screen, that he was guilty and that I knew it. They told me things would be much easier if I told them everything.

A week or so earlier, in a conversation with one of the officers there, I had been told that a psychotic would not set off the needle of a lie detector test, because they would feel no remorse or guilt. So right up front, I knew I was being lied to.

They questioned me at length.

I felt the entire time like I was wrapped in a bubble of protection. When the officer leaned aggressively toward me, he would stop short of that invisible barrier. My mind was exceptionally clear and I was in no way intimidated by their behavior. At one point, I thought to tell them that Ken loved little Theresa so much that he had brought her to our bed so we could sleep.

I felt an invisible hand cover my mouth to hold back the words.

Little did I know that at the same time, in Newport News, Ken was being hammered with accusations of using his daughter in our bed for sexual arousal.

Ultimately, one of the detectives came forward

with his irrefutable logic, "Man is capable of anything; isn't that true?"

"Yes" I could have debated this, but I thought I knew what he meant. The other officer grabbed his tape recorder to turn it on, but thought better of it, I suspect he did not want to spoil the impact of the coming question.

"Ken is a man?"

"Yes." It was clear where he was going with this.

"Therefore, Ken could have done this. Right."

"No, Ken could not have done it!" I got the look that said I was not being logical.

"Ken would have given his life for Chrissy if he could have. He was with me. No, Ken could never have done this!"

That ended it, I thought. Detective Doe, who had promised to find who did this or die trying saw me out to my car around nine thirty. I turned to give him my usual hug, believing that he was only doing his job as he had been directed. He'd always had a more tender attitude toward us. Instead, he pulled me into a non-platonic embrace. Was he testing me further? I could not believe he would do that. I felt sick that he would make that move after all that had just transpired. I pulled away, got in my car without a word and went home to wait for Ken to be returned.

When he finally arrived, he was ready to pack his bags, leave us and go live as a hermit in the mountains. He didn't want to stigmatize us further with his presence, being perceived as such a pervert. He was absolutely serious. I called Preacher Russ, who at 3AM drove the twenty miles to our home and counseled with us. What a gift of Christian commitment. How could we have managed that night without his steadying influence and willingness to be there for us.

We might have slept a couple of hours before it was time to prepare for the work.day.Ken had arranged for a fellow employee to pick him up, since he had left his car at his office location. We left him on a street corner in the cold without a jacket. As we drove away, I heard a little voice from the backseat, with a profound depth of perception say…

"Daddy looked like he was going to cry."

Things finally settled down to an apparent normal, our routine interrupted only once or

twice a week by a call from our detectives
reminding Ken that they still thought he did it.

That was November, nine months after Chrissy
had been taken.

23

To have such lawsuits at all is a real defeat for you as Christians. Why not just accept mistreatment and leave it at that? It would be far more honoring to the Lord to let yourselves be cheated." (ICorinthians 6:7 LB)

February 13, 1976, two years had passed, we had faced down another *anniversary,* when Ken's mama in Asheboro, North Carolina called us. "What's going on? Why have they dug up Chrissy's grave?"

In the middle of this conversation an operator broke in on the line to tell us we had an emergency call. The funeral director in North Carolina had just found out we knew nothing about this exhumation of our daughter. They were profoundly apologetic, assuring us they had been told we were informed.

A second autopsy had been performed in Raleigh and she had already been reintered.

The immensity of this flagrant violation of our daughter, ourselves, our rights, our hope of somehow vindicating Ken by asking them to look for evidence that might provide proof that he was innocent was unconscionable. This was a calculated effort on the part of the Chesterfield police to psych us. We had many times requested that another autopsy be performed, hoping some evidence of semen would prove Ken's innocence. Now we had lost another opportunity to move the investigation beyond him.

The autopsy indicated there was no evidence of drugs, specifically the drugs prescribed for Theresa's epilepsy. DNA was not on the radar back then, so nothing was done to remove any selective specimens that might have helped us later.

I called the warrant issuing judge to challenge the decision to keep this travesty from us. His response to everything I said was, "Take us to court. Take us to court. Just take us to court."

I finally said, "What if this had been your little girl?"

His sarcastic reply, "That's not the point."

I said, "That is exactly the point." and hung up.

Why didn't we sue? We certainly were invited by several lawyers to do so. I believe we would have been more than successful had we chosen to take that direction, but it never seemed the right thing to do. We could not forget the efforts that were made initially to find Chrissy, the extra hours the officers of Chesterfield County donated, not giving up the search. Suing would not have corrected the personal component responsible for distorting facts to make us look guilty in the media, creating the image that we had lied or taking comments made by Ken out of context to make him appear to have a perverted mindset. It would only have provided us with a cash gratuity from their insurance company.

I wrote the following letter to Chief of Police Pitman in 1993:

As you probably remember, chances of resolution in our daughter's murder were violated from the outset. The morning Chrissy was taken, it took two and a half hours from the time we called for help before the first officer arrived. Footsteps in the snow leading away from our patio door were ignored in spite of my request to consider them. Fingerprints were taken from the sliding glass door three days later after countless hands experimented with the ease with which it could be opened when it was locked. It was four days before anyone seriously examined her bedroom for clues. In the following months, any request on our part to consider possible suspects were only nominally considered by the detective who came in the first day, judged and convicted us. We were questioned daily, in our naivety, by the "good guys," hoping always that our conversation might trigger a clue… Later to find that things we said were distorted and taken out of context back at the department.

We endured psychoanalysis by a police chosen psychiatrist, lie detector tests (that's plural), sodium pentathol and countless phone calls; Ken was taken in for questioning and held for some fourteen hours to be returned at 2AM, during which time he was told the lie that I was having affairs behind his back. I was called in to a separate place, told distortions of what was happening to him and was pressed to say something incriminating.

Our daughter was exhumed without our knowledge (though we had requested another autopsy) on the anniversary of her death. The officials in North Carolina were lied to with regard to our knowledge of the event as were the participating officials at the funeral home. In a later conversation with the media, Lt. Pekancy told a reporter, Lisa Antonnelli, that he thought Ken did it and further distorted the times that certain events occurred making it appear that we had lied. Her article was printed in a special section of the Richmond paper claiming several "unsolved" crimes in the area were really solved, but the police just couldn't prove anything.

I cannot express to you the mental and emotional anguish we have endured over the years having been so violated on top of the loss of our beautiful little girl. It is with considerable distress that even now, I contact you, knowing that whatever I say may again be twisted and distorted… but twenty years have passed and there is a man living and aging, who I believe took our child. Any hope of our vindication and your success in giving resolution to this crime hinges on the chance that we can elicit a confession from him before he dies.

I go on to name him and ask for help in confronting him before it was too late. I heard nothing back, but I believe this letter may have encouraged a younger generation of detectives to explore our "cold case."

24

*Your innocence will be clear to everyone. He
will vindicate you with the blazing light of justice
shinning down as from the noonday sun.
Rest in the Lord; wait patiently for Him to act…*
(Psalms 37:6-7 LB)

In the Fall of 1996, Ken and I started getting
calls again from the Chesterfield County Police.
We ignored them until they started calling me at
the school where I was teaching. I returned
their call to find they wanted to meet with us.

They were coming through North Carolina and
wanted to update us on our case. The woman I
spoke with assured me that Ken was no longer
a suspect and their intentions were only to bring
us up to date. Apparently two of Chesterfield's
officers had opened up our "cold case" and
followed up on a man who had been identified in
the area when Chrissy went missing and had
later been caught in the act of raping an eleven
year old in New York. These detectives
had done an extensive investigation including
tracking him throughout various stints in jail
in Nebraska, Texas and Florida and interviewing
several of his jail mates in the process. They
were on their way to Charlotte, North Carolina
with a warrant for his DNA in the hopes of
finding some kind of match with our case or
pending cases in Pennsylvania and Ohio.

We never heard back about any of the results of the DNA comparisons, and when I stopped by the Chesterfield County Police Department several years later, these two officers had long since been transferred to other duties and the detectives in charge knew nothing about any of this. That's pretty much where it rests today, but God is not finished with His work.

Their visit and sincere apology for the way we had been treated, however late, resulted in an unexpected realization on my part of how exceptionally well our children had navigated this travesty with us. Four, five and six years old when their sister was abducted, in 1996, they were in their twenties, accomplished professionals, married, responsible adults with wonderful humor and a well grounded faith. Each with their respective spouses sat in on our conference prepared to make sure no further abuse would be piled on their dad.

My enormous pride was mixed with the realization of what a miracle it took for God to bring them through their growing up years to become the healthy minded people of integrity they were.

Ken has been acknowledged as innocent by The Chesterfield County Detectives we spoke

97

with, but we await *patiently*, well sometimes impatiently, the day when God will make his innocence "clear to everyone," especially in the Richmond area.

He cannot forget the day when some man stopped in his office for a loan and asked, "What do ya think of that man who killed his little girl?!"

His answer to him, after he let him talk awhile, "Well, I'm that man, and I didn't do it." The man was embarrassed enough to just leave.

How blessed we have been, surrounded by the love and concern of our friends, in a comfortable home that has accommodated children, friends, puppies, cats and even a bird over the years. Our incomes were never affected and we have seen our children through the higher education of their choices. How very, very blessed, most of all to be loved and respected by our children!

I do appreciate all the Chesterfield County Police did that was right, their efforts initially to find our daughter, their footwork following up leads all the way from New York to Texas, Florida and the Northwest United States; and the sincerity of their apologies.

25

What a wonderful God we have - He is
theFather of our Lord Jesus Christ, the
source of every mercy, and the one who so
wonderfully comforts and strengthens
us... (2Corinthians 1:3-4 LB)

When our first grandchild was born and I had
occasion to have her all to myself, the flood of
joy in holding that miniature miracle of God
brought back to me the surprise and wonder of
the depth love I felt holding my firstborn. I
hadn't realized how much joy I had missed in
my effort to keep Chrissy alive in my grief.

I didn't understand that it did not honor her to
continue to grieve and it would not be her desire
for me. Delighting in this baby would utterly
delight and honor her.

Delight in God's creatures, puppies, kittens
honors her. When we discovered that our little
Pekingese was pregnant, she fed her each
chunk of dog kibble by hand, walked her and
mothered her. I got my joy back and with it, a
much stronger witness to the kind of loving
Savior we serve.

I have the joy and assurance that our precious
daughter is home free, wrapped in His love

forever. I have the ongoing blessings of the love of my family, and realize, as with my mother, that some people never experience the sense of being cherished in their lifetime. I think we have the most beautiful grandchildren in the world. I have pets who teach me constantly about God's unconditional love! I've been sky diving! I've learned in my sixties how to ride a motorcycle! I'm blessed with a hundredfold of blessings, pressed down and overflowing!

26
If you cling to your life, you will lose it; but if you give it up for me, you will save it.
(Matthew 10:39 LB)

From the day I seriously committed myself to Christ, He has blessed my life. He sheltered me in His House (Marywood Convent), helped me heal, grow and learn. He allowed me the privilege of teaching His children in classrooms from Michigan to California to North and South Carolina and enjoy the rewards of seeing many positive results of my time spent with them then and as I encounter them as adults.

And, now, He allows me to carry His message under the guidance of Stonecroft Ministries to Christian Women's Clubs throughout North Carolina and its neighboring States.

God wants a beautiful life for you as well. He wants to be there in your pain and rejoice with you in your delights. He wants you to know He loves you, but He won't force Himself on you.

I want to invite you to pray the following prayer if you want to receive Jesus as your Lord and Savior
and you want to spend the rest of your life in a loving relationship with Him.

Father, I come to You. I confess that I am a sinner. I believe that You sent Your Son, Jesus, to die for me so I could be forgiven my sins and spend eternal life in Your love.

I ask You to forgive me for my sins and to fill me with your Holy Spirit,

I surrender all that I have, all that I am, all that I am not to You, and ask You to be Lord of my life.

Thank You for Your love and mercy. Thank You for saving me. Thank You for all the good things You have put in my life.

Help me to always seek and know Your will, and, Father, help me in the doing of it.

In Jesus precious name. Amen

Unless we come as little children, we shall not enter into the kingdom of heaven.
(Luke 18:16 LB)

27

*…Forgive us our sins, just as we have forgiven
those who have sinned against us…*
(Matt. 6: 12 LB)

Even those who don't **deserve** it?

Oh! That would be me too.

I confess it never occured to me to forgive the
man who took Chrissy from us. But, scripture
after scripture fell into place convincing me that
it was, in fact, His will. So, driving down the
highway, as this became crystal clear to me,

I said, "All right, Father, I forgive him." I felt a
spiritual force blow out of me.

My immediate reaction was, "Wait a minute!" (I
didn't know I had a power like that in me!)

But, "No, It's Your will." I gave it to God. I don't
quite understand what happened, but I clearly
understood His will.

 I wonder why God would allow me to wake up
in the middle of the night the Saturday after
Chris was abducted, with a sense of vomiting
over and over. I wasn't sick to my stomach, I

was sensing what was happening with the man who killed my child in his remorse or realization of what he had done! Perhaps to help me understand that he, too, might have a place in Jesus' heart. Even him.

He has to live with what he has done... and die with it.

Forgiven by grace,

or not...

We are praying, too, that you will be filled with His mighty glorious strength so that you can keep going no matter what happens – always full of the joy of the Lord, and always thankful to the Father Who has made us fit to share all of the wonderful things that belong to those who live in the kingdom of light.

For He has rescued us out of the darkness and gloom of Satan's kingdom and brought us into the kingdom of His dear Son, Who bought our freedom with His blood and forgave us all our sins. (Col. 1:11 – 14 LB)

How many of us would give up even one of our children to save the others? God the Father did.
Horseplay at it's best

Chrissy with her dad

Ken and I
Chrissy
Kenny, Theresa and David

A few years ago, I headed out to get to my job
after seeing the kids all off to school.
The van wouldn't start.
So
I pitched a full blown tantrum right there in front
of God.

I informed Him of how hard I worked, took care
of my family, tried to be responsible, tried to get
to my job on time, and added in a few
expletives.
I was so mad at Him.
Ken got me to work, the world didn't come to an
end. I pouted most of the day, but…
When I got home that afternoon and confronted
the offending van,
I discovered it had a flat front tire.
Had it started that morning and had I taken it on
the road in my daily rush, that unstable old van
would surely have rolled as its tire went flat on
the highway.
Ummm.
God,
I'm so sorry. I was being such a spoiled brat,
and after all You've done for me.
I'm completely forgiven,
even though I don't deserve it.
Moreover, I'm completely loved,
even though I don't deserve it.
God! How could I let that happen?

42741374R00062

Made in the USA
Middletown, DE
20 April 2017